Fame, Blame, and the Raft of Shame

BRAVE
BOOKS

DOM-A-TRON

THE OLD ISLANDS

Burrycanter

Doomsdome

UTOPIA

Freedom Island

WIGGAMORE WOO

SUMA SAVANNA

Rushington

Hive Hav

Furenzy Park

Toke-A-Toke

Wonder Wall

Capitol

RAKA RAIN FOREST

Mushroom Village

Deserted Desert

Mt. Avalerif

SkyTree

Snapfast Meadow

CAR-A-LAGO COAST

Starlotte City

Gray Landing

Home of the Brave

Welcome to **Freedom Island**, Home of the Brave, where good battles evil and truth prevails. It's up to you to defend our great nation. Save the animals of Starlotte City by completing the BRAVE Challenge at the end of this book.

Watch this video for an introduction to the story and BRAVE universe!

Saga One: The Origins
Book 4

Fame, Blame, and the Raft of Shame

Saga One: The Origins—Book 4

Fame, Blame, and the Raft of Shame

Copyright © 2021 by BRAVE BOOKS.
All Rights Reserved.

Book Illustrations © 2021 by André Ceolin
Map Illustration © 2021 by Ali Elzeiny

Published by BRAVE BOOKS
www.BRAVEbooks.us

ISBN: 978-1-955550-03-1 (paperback)

First edition published in the USA in 2021 by BRAVE BOOKS.

Printed in Canada.

Fame, Blame, and the Raft of Shame

Dan Crenshaw and BRAVE BOOKS

Art by André Ceolin

STARLOTTE

BRAVE BOOKS

Just off of Car-a-lago Coast, deep below the ocean blue, was a wondrous place called Starlotte City. Protected underneath a seaweed dome that glowed green in the sun, the city was full of light and life.

At the tippity-top of the dome whirled a fantastical winding whirlpool, the only entrance to the grand city. Animals from across Freedom Island came to see the famous shows of Ocean Boulevard.

In this bright and bubbly city lived a hippopotamus named Eva who loved to laugh.

Ever since she was as little as a butterfly burp, Eva had dreamed of telling jokes on stage. She had only one problem ....

Eva was terrified of speaking
to a crowd.

To build courage, Eva got a job working for Swan, the most famous magician in all of Starlotte City.

Eva answered phone calls, sold tickets, and even rode all the way up the whirlpool to the beach to buy Swan's favorite sea salt coffee. And, to Eva's delight, Swan let Eva be in her magic show every night.

Eva was finally a part of the magnificent history of Ocean Boulevard, where all of Freedom Island's best performers made their names.

Eva was always tired from all the work, and it didn't help that Swan sawed her in half every night. But the opportunity was worth it.

One night, Swan asked her audience for a brave volunteer. Mr. Mountain Lion raised his big paw and leapt to the stage with a triumphant roar. The crowd cheered because he was one of Freedom Island's soldiers! But then, a skunk with a smirk called out, "Maybe the magician should pull another eye out of her hat!"

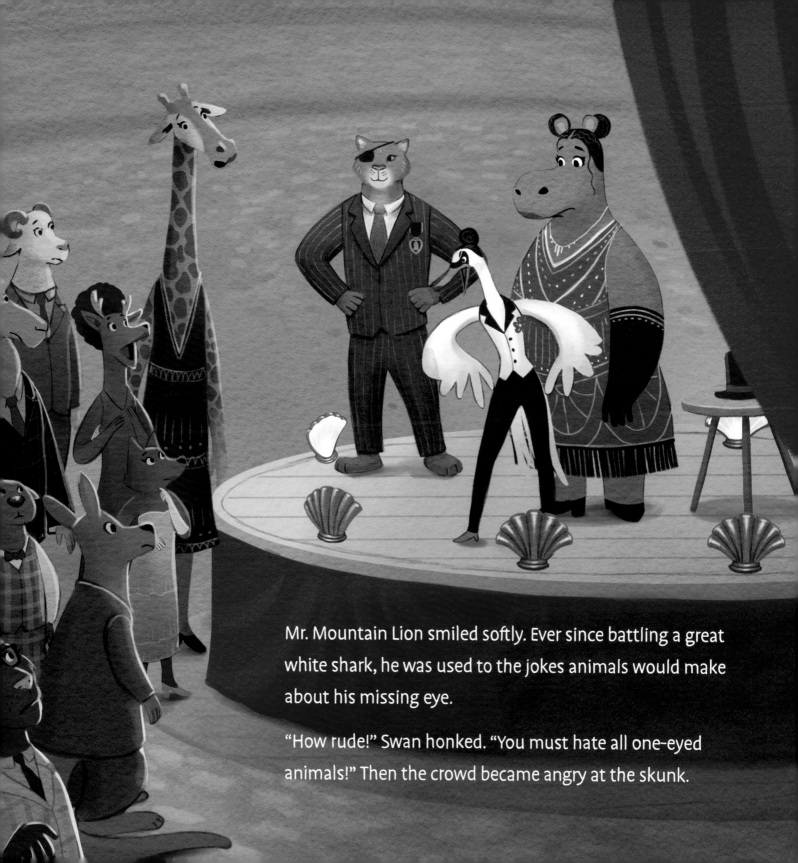

Mr. Mountain Lion smiled softly. Ever since battling a great white shark, he was used to the jokes animals would make about his missing eye.

"How rude!" Swan honked. "You must hate all one-eyed animals!" Then the crowd became angry at the skunk.

"This hateful animal has hurt Mr. Mountain Lion's feelings!" yelled Swan. "Let's build a Raft of Shame, and trap the skunk forever in the whirlpool. This way, all who visit our great city will see his shame."

"Eva, use your might to throw this skunk out. Shame on him! We don't want his hate in Starlotte City!"

"Shame, shame!" the crowd echoed.

Eva and the crowd glared at the skunk. How dare he offend Mr. Mountain Lion! With a smirk and a snort, Eva tossed him onto the Raft of Shame and hurled him up the whirlpool.

Round and round, the skunk swirled, sobbing with sorrow. "I was only joking!"

After that, shows went on, and the animals forgot about the skunk.

But whirling high above the city, the Raft of Shame pulled so hard on the dome that it cracked! Soon, water began to drip:

bloop.

blop.

bloop.

blop.

Thankfully, a seaweed
mechanic was eager to
fix the leaks.

A few nights later, right before Swan pulled Eva out of a hat, a stream of icy water went SPLAT down her back. "How rude!" Swan honked. "The beaver did that on purpose. Shame on him!"

"Shame, shame!" the crowd echoed. "Eva, use your might to throw this beaver on the Raft of Shame. We don't want his hate in Starlotte City!"

Eva knew the beaver didn't mean to get Swan wet, but the other animals glared at her. Fear tied her tongue in a knot, so with a squeak and a snort, she tossed the beaver onto a raft and hurled him up the whirlpool.

Round and round, the skunk and beaver swirled. "I was only trying to help!" the beaver cried.

Grumpy as ever, Swan banished more animals to the Raft of Shame every day. Swan banned Chipmunk for singing a song that offended her, Antelope for accidentally poking a puffer fish, and Pig just for being friends with a shark!

The Raft of Shame was so full now that the crack in the seaweed dome grew bigger, and cold seawater flooded the city. With the city's only seaweed mechanic on the Raft of Shame, no one could stop the leaks.

Then, one night, Swan decided to stop her magic show and instead say mean things about the animals on the raft. "Look at all the water that fell through the dome. Those animals deserved to be banished!"

No one in the crowd made a peep, but Eva laughed to herself. "That's ridiculous!"

"What are you laughing at, you ugly hippopotamus?" demanded Swan.

"Come tell the crowd what's so funny."

Fear tied Eva's tongue in a knot, and she began to **shake**.

Eva thought of the poor, cold animals on the raft. She had to speak.

"If you punish animals you think are hateful by being hateful to them, doesn't that make you hateful too? Swan, your actions make about as much sense as a snorkel on a fish."

The animals howled with laughter.

Ha Ha Ha Ha!

Ah Ha Ha!

"Eva is being mean!" cried Swan. "Let's send her to the Raft of Shame!"

"No!" yelled the crowd. "We should put Swan on a raft! Shame, shame! Eva, use your might to throw Swan onto the Raft of Shame. We don't want her hate in Starlotte City!"

"Enough!" said Eva. "If we put Swan on the raft, we're just as mean as she is. Instead of banishing animals when they say mean things, we can choose not to listen to them."

So with a grin and a grunt,
Eva pulled the raft down the
winding whirlpool.

Eva and the crowd apologized for sending the animals to the raft when they knew it was wrong. "We should try hard not to offend others," Eva said, "but we should try even harder not to be offended. This will make us all stronger."

"Skunk," said Mr. Mountain Lion, "I forgive you. It may have been a bad joke, but I know you didn't mean to hurt me."

After Beaver repaired the city, Eva moved the Raft of Shame to the middle of the city and called it the Stage of Fortitude. Her first act was a funny show with the skunk and Mr. Mountain Lion. It was the most popular performance of the year!

No one wanted to listen to Swan's angry honking anymore, and soon, she had to find another job taking calls, selling tickets, and buying sea salt coffee for Starlotte's new favorite joke teller: a certain hippopotamus named Eva, who loved to laugh.

A few weeks later, Eva accepted a mysterious invitation ....

Dear Eva,

Often, the strongest among us show strength not by yelling but by laughing.

Your bravery in seeking justice in Starlotte City has come to our attention, and we salute you. Freedom Island needs help from animals who are strong of heart like you. If you are willing to defend our dear island, answer the call. Journey to Wizards Way by the first day of fall.

Hurry. Our island will not last long without heroes to defend her.

Anticipating your speedy arrival—
The Legends of Freedom Island

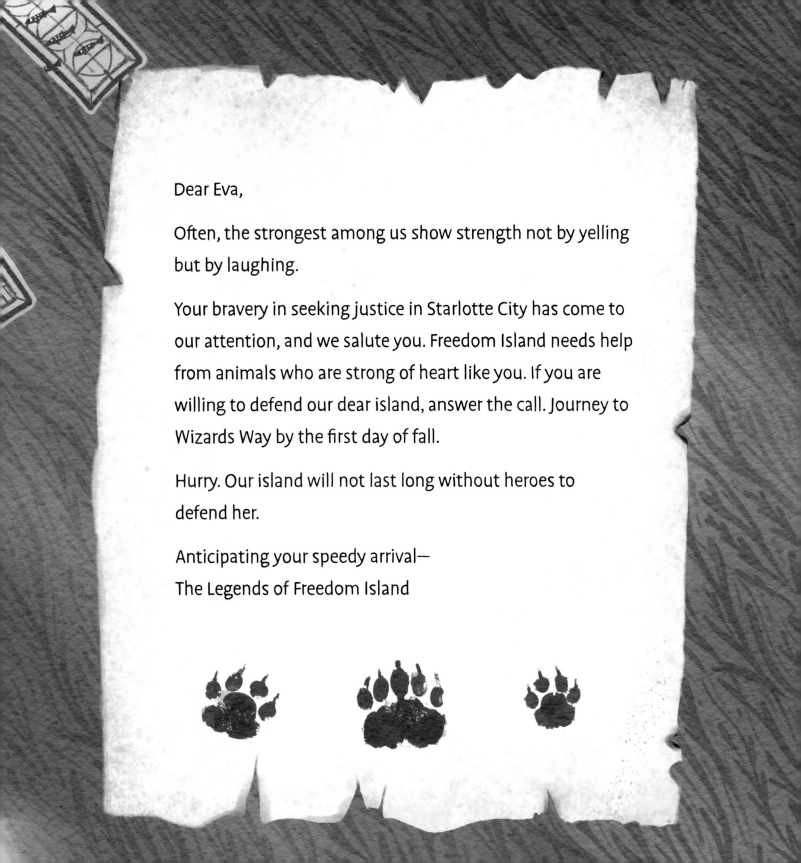

TO YOUR FAMILY

INTRODUCTION

BRAVE Books has created the BRAVE Challenge to drive home key lessons and values illustrated in the storybook. Each activity (a game and the accompanying discussion questions) takes between 10 and 20 minutes. Family-focused and collaborative, the BRAVE Challenge is a quick and fun option for family game night.

BRAVE CHALLENGE KEY

 Read aloud to the children

 One child modification

 For parents only

 Roll the die for Team Swan

THE BRAVE CHALLENGE

 ## OBJECTIVE

Welcome to Team BRAVE! Your mission for this BRAVE Challenge is to save the animals in Starlotte City from being cancelled by Swan. To get started, grab a sheet of paper and a pencil, then draw a scoreboard titled Team BRAVE vs. Team Swan, like the one shown.

Team Swan	Team BRAVE
|||	⊬⊬ ||

While the children create the scoreboard, decide on a reward for victory. Here are a few ideas:

- *Hosting a family talent show*
- *Movie night*
- *Playing the children's favorite game*
- *Going swimming*
- *Buying candy bars*
- *Riding bikes*
- *Whatever gets your kiddos excited!*

 # HOW TO PLAY

In this BRAVE Challenge, Team BRAVE (the children) will compete against Team Swan to earn points. At the end of all three activities, the team with the most points wins.

During each game the parent will roll a die for Swan. The number rolled will represent the number of points Swan earned in that game. Write this value on Swan's half of the scoreboard.

As you follow the instructions, Team BRAVE will also earn points. At the end of each game, we will write that value on the scoreboard under "Team BRAVE."

 # WINNING

At the end, if Team BRAVE has earned more points than Swan, then they have successfully saved the animals in Starlotte City. The prize for winning will be _____. Let's begin!

INTRODUCING...

DAN CRENSHAW

Dan Crenshaw is a US Congressman and conservative icon who has spent his career bringing awareness to issues close to his heart, including free speech, patriotism, and personal fortitude. He helped BRAVE Books write this story and the BRAVE Challenge and will be popping in to give you ideas on how you can explain these concepts to your child.

DAN SUGGESTS

"Hi, parents! We hope this book is a blessing to you and your family. You must protect the animals of Starlotte City against Swan! Have fun with the BRAVE Challenge!"

GAME #1 – GET ME OFF THIS RAFT!

LESSON

How to forgive, how to ask for forgiveness, and how to understand each other's intentions.

MATERIALS NEEDED

A six-sided die and one pillow per child.

Video Tutorial

 # OBJECTIVE

You are an animal living a peaceful life in Starlotte City, until one day you get thrown out and tied onto the Raft of Shame. Your objective is to make such a strong plea to the other animals of Starlotte City that they let you back in.

INSTRUCTIONS

 Before starting, roll the die to see how many points Team Swan earned. **Record this number on the scoreboard.**

Swan (parents) will come up with some unreasonable and funny reason for each child to be sent to the Raft of Shame (the pillow they stand on).

 Example ideas

- *Kid 1 has stinky feet*
- *Kid 2 called sibling "a smelly toot"*
- *Kid 3 drew a fake mustache on the dog*
- *Kid 4 is wearing a yellow shirt, and you just don't like yellow*

Team BRAVE members will have to stand on their Raft without falling off and make a plea to Swan to let them come back from the Raft of Shame.

 ## DAN SUGGESTS

"Encourage children to think about Swan's perspective, and then make a persuasive case to her. For example, "I didn't know my feet were stinky, and I would have cleaned them if you'd just told me nicely.""

Parents will award points for how good the plea is, how animated the child gets, and whether the child can stay on his or her Raft.

They can award anywhere from zero, up to eight points for a great plea. Take the average of all the kids' points, and write it on the scoreboard.

Game on!

 # TALK ABOUT IT

1. How did you feel about getting blamed for something unreasonable? What is your first response when you get blamed for something?

2. Has someone ever been upset with you and ignored you or even stopped being around you? How did this make you feel? Would you want to make someone else feel like this?

3. How should you respond to Swan when she disagrees with you?

 ### DAN SUGGESTS

"A productive society doesn't close off conversation but is open to a variety of ideas and suggestions. While we may disagree, we should have the right to express our thoughts."

"Know this, my beloved brothers: let every person be quick to hear, slow to speak, slow to anger."
James 1:19 (ESV)

4. Why was pleading while you were on the raft difficult? How do you think Skunk and Beaver from the story felt after they were sent to the Raft of Shame (canceled)? How else could those situations have been handled?

Canceling: To call out an "offensive" behavior, remark, or/and action, and to reject the person responsible through shunning or verbally targeting, as opposed to constructive and empathetic dialogue.

Cancel Culture: The cultural habit of purposefully finding offense where none should exist (such as removing Aunt Jemimah from the syrup brand). Also, accusing another of bad intentions when there are none, usually over an innocent mistake.

DAN SUGGESTS

"We all make mistakes, often unintentionally. We improve by learning from mistakes. When people get "cancelled," they are not given a chance to learn or improve. Remember: we should try hard not to offend, and try even harder not to be offended."

5. Why is communication important in a family? How about in our country?

GAME #2 - OPERATION RAFT RESCUE

LESSON

Help others using constructive feedback instead of tearing them down.

MATERIALS NEEDED

A six-sided die, three stuffed animals, and one blindfold per child.

Video Tutorial

 ## OBJECTIVE

Animals of Starlotte City are in trouble! Team BRAVE must rescue the animals canceled by Swan, who has hidden them. Navy SEALs like Dan are experts at rescuing people from dangerous situations. You can do it too!

 ## INSTRUCTIONS

 Roll the die to see how many points Team Swan earned. **Record this number on the scoreboard.**

Every member of Team BRAVE will be blindfolded and will work together to rescue three stuffed animals that are hidden around the room. For every stuffed animal rescued, Team BRAVE will be awarded two points. The game has two rounds, so you'll get two chances to find the animals. Each round will last 60 seconds.

 Round 1: *Swan (a parent) is giving instructions that are misleading and/or incorrect. Swan is also saying how bad they are doing and how they should just quit.*

Round 2: *This time, Eva (also played by a parent) is giving good instructions, positive feedback, and helpful advice. Try changing up your voice while playing the different characters.*

Game on!

TALK ABOUT IT

1. Which round was easier, the round with Swan or the round with Eva? Why?

2. Why don't people always try to give helpful feedback?

 ### DAN SUGGESTS

"Sometimes in life, people choose to tear others down in an effort to build themselves up. It's important to give healthy criticism while not being needlessly critical."

3. Sometimes during round one, Swan even said things that weren't true. It's always important to tell the truth, but it's just as important to speak with kindness. What happens when you have truth without kindness or kindness without truth?

"Do not let kindness and truth leave you; bind them around your neck,
write them on the tablet of your heart."
Proverbs 3:3 (NASB)

DAN SUGGESTS

"Kindness without truth can lead to naivete and lack of preparedness for the future (example, participation trophies). Truth without kindness can lead to demoralization (example, "Your performance was terrible. Were you even trying?"). Good communication has a proper balance of truth and kindness (example, "You lost this time, but I bet you'll work even harder and win it next time!")"

4. Can you think of anyone who speaks into your life with kindness and truth?

GAME #3 - THE BIG LAUGH CHALLENGE

LESSON

Canceling shuts down and isolates, but laughter brings joy and communion.

MATERIALS NEEDED

An open space in your living room.

Video Tutorial

 ## OBJECTIVE

Welcome to Ocean Boulevard, where Swan is about to perform. The mission for Team BRAVE is to refrain from laughing at Swan's (a parent) performance. It's up to you to keep from cracking even a smile. Join together in this mission of standing up against Swan!

INSTRUCTIONS

Have a parent stand on a "stage" by setting aside a place in the living room, in front of everyone. For example, Swan could tell these jokes:

- What does a cloud wear under his raincoat? *Thunderwear.*
- What did one toilet say to the other? *You look a bit flushed.*
- Why did the kid bring a ladder to school? *Because she wanted to go to high school.*
- What does a cow drink in the morning? *Cow-fee*
- How do you talk to a giant? *Use big words.*
- What's brown and sticky? *A twig.*

Team BRAVE earns points by refraining from laughing at Swan's jokes. Team BRAVE starts with 6 points and loses a point each time they laugh or smile during Swan's act.

Game on!

BRAVE TIP

 If a member of Team BRAVE has a joke, and Swan laughs, they can earn an additional 2 points.

TALK ABOUT IT

1. Jokes and laughter bring joy, even when you try hard not to laugh. How do you feel when you tell a joke and make people laugh?

2. Why are things like kindness, patience, and joy important?

> "But the fruit of the Spirit is love, joy, peace, patience, kindness, goodness, faithfulness, gentleness, self-control ...."
> **Galatians 5:22-23** (ESV)

1. In the book, did Eva get mad when Swan was acting rudely? How did she react? *(With laughter!)* How should you react to rude people you meet?

4. Swan wanted to cancel Eva for making a joke about her that she didn't agree with. When people disagree with you, should you shut them out of your life or try to include them? Why?

DAN SUGGESTS

"Swan tried to send Eva to the Raft of Shame, but Eva refused to do the same thing to Swan. Instead, Eva put a stop to the endless cancelling. Cancel culture is the process of bypassing normal conversation and debate, ending the discussion instead of starting it. Talk to your children about the idea of finding many different solutions to difficult problems."

"But love your enemies, and do good, and lend, expecting nothing in return, and your reward will be great, and you will be sons of the Most High, for he is kind to the ungrateful and the evil."

Luke 6:35 (ESV)

5. Luke 6:35 talks about being kind, even to your enemies. What are some benefits of being kind to people who say something you don't like?

DAN SUGGESTS

"When we show kindness in the face of cruelty it gives us the opportunity to break down divisions. We avoid unnecessary conflict, and can even start a friendship. This doesn't mean you shouldn't stand up for yourself, but you should do so with grace and fortitude, not bitterness and contempt."

TALLY ALL THE POINTS TO SEE WHO WON!

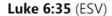

Submit comments to: Feedback@BRAVE.us